AF602016

Sacré-Coeur

France

St. Patrick's Cathedral

USA

St. Mark’s Basilica

Italy

Las Lajas Sanctuary

Colombia

Wieskirche

Germany

Church of St. George

Ethiopia

Church of the Assumption

Slovenia

Notre-Dame Basilica

Canada

Cathedral of Brasília

Brazil

Borgund Stave Church

Norway

Mont-Saint-Michel Abbey

France

Westminster Abbey

United Kingdom

St. Alexander Nevsky Cathedral

Bulgaria

Hallgrimskirkja

Iceland

St. Stephen's Cathedral

Austria

Hagia Sophia

Turkey

Kölner Dom

Germany

Catedral Basílica Del Pilar

Spain

St. Stephen’s Basilica

Hungary

Duomo di Milano

Italy

St. Peter's Basilica

Vatican City

St. John's Co-Cathedral

Malta

Santa Maria del Fiore

Italy

Notre-Dame de Paris

France

St. Basil's Cathedral

Russia

Chapel of St. Gildas

France

Basilica de Higuey

Dominican Republic

Cathedral of Rio de Janeiro

Brazil

Paoay Church

Philippines

St. Michael’s Ministry

Ukraine

Grundtvig's Church

Denmark

The Felsenkirche

Germany

Chapel in the Rock

America

Saint-Michel d’Aiguilhe chapel

France

Chapel on the Rock

America

Gergeti Trinity Church

Georgia

Church of the Transfiguration

Republic of Karelia

La Sagrada Família

Spain

Monasteries of Meteora

Greece

St. Augustine Church

United Kingdom

www.ingramcontent.com/pod-product-compliance
Ingram Content Group UK Ltd.
Pitfield, Milton Keynes, MK11 3LW, UK
UKHW060112300726
14090UKWH00002B/147

* 9 7 8 9 1 8 9 7 0 0 1 4 7 *